PAUSE TO SELAH

Benefitting from times of pause in your life

Marie Le Maitre

DM Briers Books and Publishing

Copyright © 2021 Marie Le Maitre

All rights reserved

No part of this book may be reproduced, or stored in a retrieval system, or transmitted in any form or by any means, electronic, mechanical, photocopying, recording, or otherwise, without express written permission of the publisher.

ISBN-13: 978-1-77637-895-1

Cover design by: DM Briers Books and Publishing
Library of Congress Control Number: 2018675309
Printed in the United States of America

WHAT OTHERS ARE SAYING

The heart of Marie le Maitre has always been to equip the body of Christ. In her book, she shares valuable truths that will encourage any disciple of Christ. She imparts what she received and learned from her walk of an intimate relationship with the Lord. We commend her for her love and dedication to the Lord and His people.
Snr. Pastors Kobus and Ronel van der Merwe. Midvaal Christian Centre. South Africa.

Robert E Coleman said: "Somehow, ecclesiastical programs and membership promotions have been mistaken for fulfilling the Great Commission." This book will benefit the ministry of anyone who aims to fulfill that commission, namely to make disciples.

Churches should be filled with zealous mature believers, but instead, many dedicated children of God struggle with fear, pride, anger, and unforgiveness and don't know how to deal with disappointment. Whether you are a new convert or committed leader in a discipleship group, this book provides invaluable lessons from a Biblical perspective, challenges deep-seated belief systems, and gives new spiritual insights in leading a victorious life in Christ.

Pastor Marie le Maitre is an active pastor who teaches through personal experience and important lessons learned in ministry and succeeds in equipping the body of Christ with this excellent book.

Dr./Pastor Hanli Botha, Midvaal Christian Centre, Gauteng, South Africa.

What an encouraging book, filled with truths from God's Word. I have known Marie le Maitre for many years, and we were blessed enough to have her teach at The Net of Christ Christian School (Hope Christian Academy). During her time with us, her love for the Lord and His Word and her passion for the children and people she worked with were very evident, as well as in all she did. I highly recommend her book as there are many truths and life lessons to be learned, which are very relevant for this time.

Pastor Lawrence Oosthuizen, Hope Family Church, Gauteng, South Africa.

ACKNOWLEDGMENTS

Many life events, disciple groups, friends, and Spiritual leaders contributed to me writing this book.

I am so grateful for my spiritual oversight of the last 18 years, Pastors Kobus and Ronel van der Merwe, under whom I have been serving all these years, for the confidence you have placed in me as a leader of our church, Midvaal Christian Centre.

My mother taught me to love reading and do creative writing; here's to you, mom!

Special thanks to my discipleship friends, you know who you are, for your impartation and support! You have helped me tremendously and continue to help me grow spiritually.

Then there is Danielle Briers, who encouraged me to write this book. She proved that all things are possible if you only believe and put your faith into action. Not only did she spur me on, but she also helped me with the editing and designing of the cover. I thank God that He placed you in my life just at the right time.

To Esté Nienaber, who took the pictures to cover my books in Israel – I genuinely appreciate you so much. Thank you for encouraging me to follow my dream whenever I felt like quitting.

Thanks to my daughter, who have been such a blessing during the Lockdown. I've learned so much from you, Marlize. You have been my support and spiritual inspiration throughout this time.

Special thanks to my wonderful husband, who always believes in me and never complained about me, spending time writing even late at night.

MARIE LE MAITRE

Most of all, I honor and praise the Lord for being my biggest fan. Without You, I am nothing!

INTRODUCTION

The COVID 19 pandemic of 2020 had a detrimental effect on the world.

This time will be remembered as a tremendous pause in most of our lives.

Because of this, various adjustments had to be made.

A lot of companies sent their people home to do their work from home. The schools and tertiary institutions sent the students home to do online studies, churches were closed, and believers worshiped the Lord in isolation.

Nursing homes were restricted because of the health risk, and patients in hospitals were not allowed visitors.

Due to this, we were all greatly influenced by this pandemic. The question remains: How do you deal with uncertain times like this?

As part of a full-time ministry team of MIDVAAL CHRISTIAN CENTRE in Gauteng, South Africa, our lives also came to a halt. Suddenly the business of ministry faded and a time of introspection and soul searching came. In the beginning, I enjoyed the extra time spent in the presence of the Lord and the precious time with close family. God restored – not only me personally – giving me time to deal with the disappointments and hurt of the ministry and revived neglected relationships. But then the frustration and discontentment came. I began searching the Lord for the way forward. In my search for answers, I had a dream in the early hours of the morning. I saw our church walls broken down to the ground.

Apart from the pillars in the building's corners, only the last two rows of bricks were left. Some of the church members collected the bricks and rebuilt the walls, but I could sense a hesitancy to follow. Jesus was standing next to me, and I required of him: "Lord, must we start rebuilding the walls?" He replied: "To receive the new you, need to tear down the old. Extend the foundation!" I saw Jesus standing with a new building plan in his hands – it was the blueprint for our church. He spoke to me out of Scripture: Isaiah 54:2 (TLV) *'Enlarge the place of your tent, stretch out your tabernacle curtains. Do not hold back—lengthen your cords, strengthen your stakes. For you will spread out to the right hand and the left. Your offspring will possess the nations and will resettle the desolate cities.'*

Holy Spirit revealed to me that He is allowing this great pause for us to go back to the original plan Jesus had for his church in the book of Acts. He had a far more fantastic plan than the church building ever could contain. He had to break down old thoughts and behavior patterns to build the new. Since many of us were stuck in a work pattern and neglected prayer, our hearts had to take a pause. This pause was needed for our souls to start connecting to the beginning. To connect to where the core of God lay.

I came to realize – **WHAT YOU DO IN ISOLATION COUNTS MORE THAN ACCOMPLISHMENTS ACHIEVED ON PUBLIC PLATFORMS**, and I began searching for God's will for my life even more.

Now, after almost a year of Lockdown, I concluded that THE TRUE DEPOSIT AND CHANGE HAPPEN IN ISOLATION, but there is a precondition – we need to draw near to God so that He will draw near to us (James 4:7) to speak to us.

The sad part is that most children of God don't draw near to him but instead run towards other distractions like work, money, hobbies, recreational activities, and abusive substances. On the contrary, there is an excellent reward for those who diligently seek Him and know that He is a Rewarder of those who do.

Isolation is something all human beings go through and is part of life, but how we handle these times of pause in our lives matters most. These pauses or times of reset can include a time of grieving or transition.

Each of those pause times allows us to reset the way we look at a situation. Reset used as a verb (used with object) means 'to set again: to reset an alarm clock; to reset a broken bone; to set; adjust, or fix in a new or different way: to reset priorities; to reset prices. (www.dictionary.com).

We are all afraid of change and reset because it brings us into the unknown, where we cannot plan or use our daily notes and checklist, where we cannot perform a prepared speech. But it is there, in the unknown, where things like daily planners fall to pieces, and you need to rely on prayer and God's voice to be able to move forward and know what to do next. It is what reset brings us back to.

I also refer to these 'reset' moments as 'selah'-times (as discussed in the life of David in Chapter 3). 'Selah' means, in short, to pause to reflect on the deeper meaning of a specific Scripture verse before you continue reading the rest. I urge you, therefore, to pause and reflect deeply on your walk with God as you continue reading this book. Take time to think, adjust your thoughts and actions as you study each chapter, and allow the Holy Spirit to transform you and enable you to bear much fruit to the glory of our Father.

In this book, I will also focus on a few Bible characters that went through a series of pause times in their lives, and hopefully, it will challenge your perspective and reset the way you think. These characters reveal to us how the pauses should be handled and others how they should not be handled, and in each case, there are lessons to be learned.

This book can be effectively used as a manual individually, but even more helpful in disciple - or life groups. I encourage you to answer the questions at the end of each chapter honestly.

CHAPTER 1

Noah – Obedient, Crucial Pause

One of the most well-known stories in the Old Testament is about Noah's life, who built an ark that saved himself and his family and representatives of every land animal from a great flood that God sent in judgment upon the earth.

Shortly after Noah turned 500 (before the flood, people lived many hundreds of years), God commanded Noah to build the ark, and after his 600th birthday, Noah, along with his wife, sons, and daughters-in-law, entered the Ark as God tore open the floodgates of heaven. (Genesis 7:6)
Interestingly, Noah's grandfather, Methuselah, who died in the same year as the flood, at 969 years, was the oldest man mentioned in the Bible!

Most Bible commentaries state that Noah and his family were stuck on the ark for approximately one year! No wonder Noah's name means "rest." (It derives from the Hebrew נוח (nuah), to rest.) He was forced to rest from his previous works with nowhere to go! What is even more significant; is that God shut the door of the Ark. The door refers to the Scripture in John 10:9 where Jesus said, "I am the door. If anyone enters by Me, he will be saved." Only those who believe with their heart and confess with their mouths that Jesus is the only way to the Father goes through the doorway. Romans 10:9 (TPT) *'And what is God's "living message"? It is the revelation of faith for salvation, which is the message that we preach. For if you publicly declare with your mouth that Jesus is Lord and believe in your heart that God raised him from the dead, you will experience salvation.'*

Nothing we can do will save us from our sinful nature —salvation is all of God. Our lives should be worship; our actions and words should worship out that we know Him, that He lives here. Our responsibility is to go through the doorway, which is Jesus, and God will save us.

"By grace, you have been saved through faith, and that not of yourselves; it is the gift of God" (Ephesians 2:8)."

Grace is not a topic or subject matter. It is a person, and His name is Jesus!"

For those of us with a religious background, this may be difficult to accept. We were taught to obey the law and "work" for our salvation.

I remember in Sunday school, we were taught to memorize and live according to the law, and I can still recall how many times I failed and therefore felt so unworthy to enter God's presence.

Noah's story teaches us to rest from our efforts and surrenders wholeheartedly to the Lord Jesus and trust in His salvation in our lives. Grace has invited us to come and take a seat, to rest in the finished work of Jesus. Nothing we do can ever earn our salvation.

Isaiah 64:5 (MKJV) *'For all of us have become like one who is unclean, and all our righteousness is like a filthy garment, and all of us wither like a leaf, and our iniquities carry us away, like the wind.'*
God flooded the earth because of human wickedness shows that God is a just and holy God that punishes sin and shows mercy to the righteous.
Gen 6:1 - 4 (TLV) *'Now when humankind began to multiply on the face of the ground and daughters were born to them, then the sons of God saw that the daughters of men were good and they took for themselves wives, any they chose. Then Adonai said, "My Spirit will not remain with humankind forever, since they are flesh. So their days will be 120 years." The Nephilim were on the earth in those days and afterward, whenever the sons of God came to the daughters of men and gave birth to them. Those were the mighty men of old, men of renown. When*

Adonai saw that the wickedness of humankind was great on the earth and that every inclination of the thoughts of their heart was only evil all the time. So Adonai regretted that He made humankind on the earth, and His heart was deeply pained. So, Adonai said, "I will wipe out humankind, whom I have created, from the face of the ground, from humankind to livestock, crawling things and the flying creatures of the sky, because I regret that I made them." But Noah found favor in Adonai's eyes.'

The question is – if God looks upon the earth today, will he find you righteous?

Will you find yourself in his "ark" of salvation? This is one of the most important questions we need to ask ourselves.

Nicodemus, a ruler and Jewish Pharisee asked Jesus: *"How can a man be born when he is old?" Nicodemus said to Him. "He cannot enter his mother's womb a second time and be born, can he?"* (John 3:4 (TLV)) It was after Jesus told him that you need to be born again to enter the Kingdom of God.

This remains one of the greatest mysteries of all time. John 3:5 (TLV) Yeshua *answered, "Amen, amen I tell you, unless one is born of water and spirit, he cannot enter the kingdom of God."*

If Jesus knocks on the door of your heart, will you open your heart and invite Him in?

Take time to ask yourself these questions, and if you've never done this before, ask Jesus to come into your life and fill your heart with His Spirit. Surrender your will to Him. "Great faith does not come out of great effort, but by great sacrifice" (Bill Johnson).

Confess your sins and ask forgiveness. Confess out loud that Jesus died for your sins, but that He also rose and ascended to heaven to prepare a place for you.

Believe with your heart that your new life has started now and that you are a new creation. Your heart is of royal treasure, and therefore it is essential to 'need' God to confess, to repent so that this royal treasure of yours may be used to guide other lost souls home so they can also acknowledge and repent.

2Corinthians 5:17,18 (TPT) *'Now, he has become an entirely new creation if anyone is enfolded into Christ. All that is related to the old order has vanished. Behold, everything is fresh and new. And God has made all things new, and reconciled us to himself, and given us the ministry of reconciling others to God.'*

Now you become part of the New Covenant. Just as God made a covenant with Noah and his sons (He set a rainbow in the clouds as a token), promising never to destroy them, their descendants, nor any living creatures through a flood ever again (Genesis 9:9-11), He gives His born-again children the promise of eternal life. Earth is not your home. Eternal life with Jesus in Heaven is.

I also believe that God uses disciples -, cell- or life groups right across the globe as "arks" or places of safety, especially when trouble comes. When churches come under attack, as we experienced during the COVID-19 – epidemic, the churches positioned to gather in secret small groups are more likely to survive and still grow in the most challenging times. The Lord has always been famous for hiding His children in times of calamity. Not only was Noah's family hidden in a place of safety, but He also hid Moses in the Nile river when the Hebrew baby boys' lives were threatened. He hid Elijah in a cave when Jezebel threatened to kill the prophets. He hid the nation Israel in caves when the Philistines fought against them (1 Samuel 13:6).

Today he still hides His children in underground house churches where Christian gatherings are forbidden. Governments may try to use legislations to hinder the spread of the Gospel and may think that they will defeat Christianity.

Yet, it is interesting to note that the fastest growing churches are in the previously Muslim or Hindu nations in Asia (Nepal, China, United Arab Emirates, Saudi Arabia, Qatar), where Christianity is forbidden, and people gather in secret.

Persecution and isolation have never killed the church; instead, it activates the Kingdom to spread like yeast. 'Then he *taught them another parable: "Heaven's kingdom realm can be compared to yeast that a woman takes and blends into three measures of flour and then waits until all the dough rises."* Matt. 13:33 (TPT). Praise God who works behind the scenes where nobody can see! His wisdom isn't our wisdom; His ways are higher than ours!

Lessons we can learn from Noah:

1. We ought to be inspired by Noah's life to build our faith also to do mighty exploits. Daniel 11:32 (NKJV) '*Those who do wickedly against the covenant he shall corrupt with flattery; but the people who know their God shall be strong, and carry out great exploits.*' We get to know our God by spending time in His presence and His Word so that our Spirit man grows stronger. Like Noah, we can also have his unmovable faith and godly fear, leading us to be obedient to whatever God commands us to do!"*Faith opened Noah's heart to receive revelation and warnings from God about what was coming, even things that had never been seen. But he stepped out in reverent obedience to God and built an ark that would save him and his family. By his faith, the world was condemned, but Noah received God's gift of righteousness that comes by believing.* (Hebrews 11:7(TPT)). Note that Noah is numbered as being amongst three of the most righteous men in the book of Ezekiel, alongside Job and Daniel:"*As surely as I live, declares the Sovereign LORD, even if Noah, Daniel, and Job were in it, they could save neither son nor daughter. They would save only themselves by their righteousness*" (Ezekiel 14:20 (NIV)).

2. We can leave a legacy for our children and their children's children. Just like Noah did. His family of 8 people: Noah, his wife, three sons, and their wives were the only human survivors of the flood and became the founders of a new and second lineage of humanity that brought about our salvation in Jesus Christ. These events leading up to the flood can be seen as a forerunner for the second coming of Jesus Christ (Matthew 24:37-39).

3. Eight speaks of covenant promises. Being in a covenant relationship with Jesus gives us the security that He fights for us and will lead us through the most challenging times

4. God promises never to leave nor forsake us! He will hide His children from calamity and protect us from harm. (Psalm 91)

5. We are not just saved for ourselves – God always has someone else in mind whose life you can touch.

Questions:

Read Genesis 6 – 10

1. Testify of your salvation. What proof do you have that you are born again?
2. How does the life of Noah inspire you?
3. What inheritance do you want to leave behind as a child of God?

CHAPTER 2

Joseph – Unfairly Isolated

Have you ever been misunderstood or falsely accused? Then the story of Joseph in Genesis 37 – 50 is written for you.

We find the young seventeen-year-old boy sharing his dream of him and his brothers out in the field, tying up bundles of grain, and his bundle stood up, and his brother's bundles all gathered around and bowed before his (Genesis 37:5,6), which made them very jealous.

After telling them the following dream in which the sun, moon, and eleven stars bowed low before him (Genesis 37:9), – it was the last straw, and they planned to kill him, but when one of his brothers, Reuben, heard about it, he convinced them not to kill him but throw him into an empty cistern.

We read how they ripped off the beautiful robe his Father made him, grabbed him, and threw him into the cistern. They sold him to a group of Ishmaelite traders that came by and took him to Egypt. Talk about innocently being treated with contempt and hatred!

The story continues where the traders sold Joseph to Potiphar, the captain of the palace guard. Potiphar soon realized that the Lord was with Joseph because he succeeded in everything he did, and he soon made Joseph his attendant and put him in charge of his entire household and everything he owns.

He was quickly given all the administrative responsibilities over all of Potiphar's affairs. Because Joseph was handsome and well-built, Potiphar's wife began looking at him lustfully and demanded that he sleep with her. Joseph's godly, stable character is displayed as he rejected her request even after pressuring him day after day.

Then the story gets to a breakpoint where Potiphar's wife one day grabbed him by his cloak and demanded that he sleep with her. 'She caught him by his cloak and said, *"Come to bed with me!" But he left his cloak in her hand and ran out of the house.'* (Genesis 39:12 (NIV) What happened next is what caused the great pause in Joseph's life! He was accused of trying to rape Potiphar's wife. Potiphar was furious and had him thrown into prison.

What makes this story so memorable is how Joseph handled the pauses or isolation in his life. He kept staying true to who he was. He remained steadfast and humble. He didn't give in to compromise. He never tried to defend himself or give in to self-pity.

We see how he was again handled unfairly, mistreated, and thrown in prison. And again, how did he respond?

How would you respond when repeatedly treated unfairly?

In prison, Joseph still had this unequaled favor upon his life. We read in Genesis 40 and how he interpreted the cup-bearer and chief baker's dreams. He then asked the cup-bearer, *"But when all goes well with you, remember me and show me kindness; mention me to Pharaoh and get me out of this prison."* (Genesis 40:14 NIV)

Shortly afterward, Joseph's interpretations became true when Pharaoh had a birthday banquet and summoned his chief cup-bearer and chief baker to join the other officials. *'He then restored the chief cupbearer to his position, so he once again put the cup into Pharaoh's hand, but he hanged the chief baker, just as Joseph had said to them in his interpretation. The chief cupbearer, however, did not remember Joseph. He forgot him.'* (Genesis 40:21 – 23 (NIV))

Just imagine the turmoil that might have been in his thoughts – Why did the cup-bearer not adhere to his promise? How could he forget about me? Did God also forget about me? When is this horror going to end? When will justice be done?

How would you have reacted had it been you?

What followed was a two-year pause for Joseph, still bound to prison, until Pharaoh had a dream and the cup-bearer then suddenly remembered his promise to Joseph. He then told Pharaoh, *'Now a young Hebrew was there with us, a servant of the captain of the guard. We told him our dreams, and he interpreted them for us, giving each man the interpretation of his dream. And things turned out exactly as he interpreted them to us: I was restored to my position, and the other man was hanged. So, Pharaoh sent and called for Joseph, and he was quickly brought from the dungeon. When he had shaved, changed his clothes, and came before Pharaoh.'* (Genesis 41:12 – 14 (NIV))

God reminded the cup-bearer of his promise even though it took some time! Praise God for his faithfulness! Joseph had to endure and remain loyal to his character.

Joseph's story continues to teach us that God's timing is very often not our time. It was nearly 14 years between his dream and the time he left prison to become second in Egypt's command.

This pattern is found throughout the Bible, and I believe God still does it today. One of the many lessons we learn from Joseph's life is that we need to endure and stand upon his promises even if it looks impossible and maybe even a bit far-fetched.

Then this story unfolds in the most amazing act of kindness and mercy. Joseph was able to explain the meaning of Pharaoh's dream after he was released from prison. That impressed Pharaoh so much; "*So Pharaoh said to Joseph, "You shall be in charge of my palace, and all my people are to submit to your orders. Only concerning the throne will I be greater than you."* (Genesis 41:41, 42 (NIV)).

Then Pharaoh appointed Joseph over the whole of Egypt. He removed his signet ring from his hand and put it on Joseph's hand, clothed him with fine linen garments, and put a chain of gold around his neck. You would have thought that Joseph would retaliate against those who caused so much pain and agony in his life now that he had all this authority as leader over Egypt, but yet when famine broke out, and his brothers came to buy food from him, he was moved with compassion.

Genesis 42:25 (NIV) *'Joseph gave orders to fill their bags with corn, to put each man's silver back in his sack, and to give them provisions for the journey.'*

After a long series of events, Joseph revealed his true identity to his brothers. As the story unfolds, it becomes the most precious comparison of the way Jesus loves us unconditionally.

Genesis 45:1- 11 (NIV) 'Then *Joseph could no longer control himself before all his attendants, and he cried out, "Make everyone leave my presence!" So there was no one with Joseph when he made himself known to his brothers. And he wept so loudly that the Egyptians heard him, and Pharaoh's household heard about it. Joseph said to his brothers, "I am Joseph! Is my Father still living?" But his brothers were not able to answer him because they were terrified at his presence. Then Joseph said to his brothers, "Come close to me." When they had done so, he said, "I'm your brother, Joseph, the one you sold into Egypt! And now, do not be distressed and do not be angry with yourselves for selling me here because it was to save lives that God sent me ahead of you. For two years now, there has been famine in the land, and for the next five years, there will be no plowing and reaping. But God sent me ahead of you to preserve a remnant on earth and save your lives by a great deliverance. "So then, it was not you who sent me here, but God. He made me Father to Pharaoh, lord of his entire household and ruler of all Egypt. Now hurry back to my Father and say to him, 'This is what your son Joseph says: God has made me lord over all Egypt. Come down to me; don't delay. You shall live in the region of Goshen and be near me, you, your children and grandchildren, your flocks and herds, and all you have. I will provide for you there because five years of famine are still to come. Otherwise, you and your household and all that belong to you will become destitute.'*

Joseph had to work through the disappointment and grant them forgiveness before extending a hand of mercy towards his brothers, who caused so much grief in his life.

Surely he understood what David said when he cried out: Psalms 51:12 – 15 (TLV) *'Create in me a clean heart, O God, and renew a steadfast spirit within me. Do not cast me from Your presence—take not Your Ruach ha-Kodesh from me. Restore to me the joy of Your salvation and sustain me with a willing spirit. Then will I teach transgressors Your ways, and sinners will return to You.'*

Every Christian goes through these tests of forgiveness and humility. Being a pastor in full-time ministry for the last 18 years, I can testify that some of the most severe difficulties you go through, and I believe some readers can identify with some. I have been falsely accused of not being there for people in difficult times.

Yet, at the same time, I can recall how many times we have sacrificed precious times with our own family to do hospital visits. To help rescue a drug addict and taking him to a rehabilitation center in the middle of the night, cutting a boy loose from a suicide rope, try to speak sense into an alcoholic husband physically abusing his wife and her son, and the list can go on.

How many times was I tested in keeping my heart pure, forgiving, and releasing people in the most challenging times! I've learned that the pruning process is the most intense in these times. John 15 describes how we get pruned by our Father, who is the gardener. He cuts off every branch that doesn't produce fruit, and He prunes the branches that do bear fruit to have even more. True disciples are known by their fruit, and it brings great glory to the Father. The fruit of the spirit mentioned in Galatians 5: 22 is not given to us as gifts but is cultivated in testing times. Without keeping the cross and the price Jesus paid in mind, you will never be able to bear the required fruit.

James 1:2 - 4 (TPT) *'My fellow believers, when it seems as though you are facing nothing but difficulties, see it as an invaluable opportunity to experience the greatest joy that you can! For you know that when your faith is tested, it stirs up power within you to endure all things. And then as your endurance grows even stronger, it will release perfection into every part of your being until nothing is missing and nothing lacking.'*

I want to encourage you to use the following five steps to deal with your disappointment. I've used this easy method in my own life and disciple groups and have experienced breakthroughs, restoration, and healing. These steps are as follows:

Step 1: **Acknowledge your disappointment**, for example: "I'm disappointed in my boss."

Step 2: **Reflect on it. Ask "Why?" questions and discuss the answers,** for example: "He didn't keep his word; I didn't receive the raise he promised." **Why?** "The company's income didn't grow." **Why do I still feel disappointed?** "He makes me feel that I'm not worthy." **Since when have you felt this way?** "Ever since I was a little girl."

Step 3: **Write down what you realized.**

"Daddy promised he would be at the prize-giving, but he never came, and he made me feel I'm not worthy of his love."

Take control of your reactions.

Step 4: **Edit, Recheck.**

How can I make this better for that person or help resolve the relationship?

Forgive the person.

Step 5: **Take an action step.**

> Turn the disappointment into an opportunity to learn new information.
>
> For example: "Father, I always feel I'm not worthy. Thank you for showing me where I felt this way before. (Close your eyes and revisit that place of pain.) Show me what you want me to know. (Wait until the Lord reveals it to you). How can I restore or contribute to a better relationship with that person?"

Today, Joseph's life remains one of the most inspiring stories filled with relevant messages of integrity, hope, steadfast endurance, forgiveness, and restoration. Joseph's life is a shadow of how Jesus lived and encouraged us to walk in his footsteps. If our ultimate goal is not to be more like Jesus – we have the wrong gospel!

Lessons we can learn from Joseph

1. Forgive quickly, even when mistreated and without cause. Forgive like Jesus. Luke 23:34 (KJV) *'Then said Jesus, Father, forgive them; for they know not what they do. And they parted his raiment and cast lots.'*

2. Stay humble and dependant on God even when you are in an important position of authority. Joseph could have taken revenge on his brothers, yet he showed undeserved grace. He indeed was Jesus to them.

3. Don't give in to compromise. Joseph didn't take advantage of his position when Pharaoh's wife tried to seduce him. Remember your godly values when facing temptation.

4. Work through disappointment, extend a hand of mercy towards your enemies.

5. Allow God to prune you to bear more fruit.

QUESTIONS:

Read Genesis 37 - 50

1. How can you personally relate to the life of Joseph?

2. What stands out to you the most in this story?

3. How can you apply these truths in your daily life?

CHAPTER 3

David – Trained In Isolation

David, Israel's greatest king, is one of the characters in the Bible that was trained in isolation to the extent that he finally became a man after God's own heart (1 Samuel 13:14; Acts 13:22). Yet his life was filled with typical ups and downs most of us face every day. The remarkable story of King David is told in 1 Samuel 16 – 24 and 1 Kings 1 and 2.

When David was a teenager, he was anointed by the prophet Samuel as the next king of Israel, although he thought of calling Saul, who was much taller and well built. '
But the Lord said to Samuel, "Do not consider his appearance or his height, for I have rejected him. The Lord does not look at the things man looks at. Man looks at the outward appearance, but the Lord looks at the heart" (1 Samuel 16:7 (NIV).

David was out in the fields watching the sheep and goats when he was anointed as king, but it was only 15 years later that he became king. Talk about a great pause!In these years of preparation, he spent time in isolation, facing Goliath, was banished by Saul, hiding in the desert, lived on the run, was forced out of the nation, and fought many battles. He was tested, just like Joseph, so that God could convert him from a shepherd into a king. Like Joseph, his life represents many of the battles we, as children of God, also fight. Psalm 105:19 says, *"God's promise to Joseph purged his charac-*

ter until it was time for his dreams to come true." (TPT).

One thing is sure - when God puts a dream in our hearts, we will undergo a period of testing.

David's life is an excellent example of how to go through these times of testing and trials. Although Saul was jealous of David and often tried to kill him, David never retaliated. *'It came about the next day that an evil spirit from God came mightily upon Saul so that he was raving within the palace. While David was playing music with his hand, as he did day by day, Saul had his spear in his hand, and Saul hurled the spear, thinking, "I'll pin David to the wall!" But David eluded him—twice.'* (1 Sam. 18:10,11 (TLV)

More than once, David had the ideal opportunity to kill Saul, yet he always showed respect and mercy. One day Saul found himself in a cave after fighting the Philistines. David and his men hid farther back in that very cave when Saul went into it to relieve himself. He was so close to Saul that he was able to cut off a piece of the hem of his robe, yet David said in 1Samuel 24:6, 7 (TLV) ... *"Adonai forbids that I should do such a thing to my lord, Adonai's anointed, stretching out my hand against him—for he is Adonai's anointed." So David persuaded his fellow men with these words and did not let them rise against Saul. Then Saul left the cave and went on his way.'*

We are motivated by David's life to honor those in authority even when they don't deserve our respect and to submit to their authority. Maybe you are subjected to the unfair, cruel behavior of a manager you work under then learn from the life of David. One thing we can be sure of is that *'... For in this unbelieving world, you will experience trouble and sorrows, but you must be courageous, for I (Jesus) have conquered the world!'* (John 16: 33 (b) (TPT))James1:13 (TPT) also states, *"When you are tempted don't ever say, "God is tempting me," for God is incapable of being tempted by evil and he is never the source of temptation."*

We need to realize **THE GREATER THE CALLING; THE GREATER THE TEST.** God uses those tests to form our character to make sure we don't waste the calling. GOD IS MORE INTERESTED IN OUR CHARACTER THAN IN OUR CALLING. God knows when we aren't ready to handle the fulfillment, so He tests us to help us become the person who will steward the calling well.

I can recall many times in ministry when I felt led by the Holy Spirit to do certain things, but the timing was wrong. There was a time (when still serving as a group leader) when I wanted our church to start a prophet school after I came back from prophetic training in another church in Pretoria. I remember being full of zeal, driving back on the highway and landing on the wrong off-ramp that led to me on a detour. I landed behind a huge truck carrying an abnormal load and was praying and singing in the spirit.

After a while, I got so impatient with the situation that I tried to pass the truck, but as I was about to do so, traffic came from the opposite direction, and I had to slow down and got stuck behind the truck again. I heard the Holy Spirit saying: "Slow down, you are going to get hurt." Needless to say, when I suggested to our senior pastor, we start a prophet school at our church, the answer was "not now." This was not the season for us to venture in that direction. I submitted myself to the leadership of our senior pastor even though my heart was broken. I learned to honor my leadership and wait for God to open the right door. Many times the dream has to die before God resurrects it again. You have to die to your ambition and desires and allow God to work on your character. Our character truly is more important to God than our calling!

Today we do prophetic training in our church on a much broader scale than a prophet school could have done!Sadly I've seen so many people leave the church because they were not willing to lay down their visions to serve the vision of the house first. They were unwilling to serve behind the scenes like David did, being faithful until God opened the door. Ultimately God is after our hearts more than anything! He cuts away selfish pride and ambition and has ways of humbling us when we are stubborn and arrogant. It's not always easy to distinguish when a vision is selfish or prideful because it looks very sacrificial and even has a religious color.

Still, God knows our hearts better than we know ourselves. Romans 8:27 (TPT) *'God, the searcher of the heart, knows our longings fully, yet he also understands the desires of the Spirit, because the Holy Spirit passionately pleads before God for us, his holy ones, in perfect harmony with God's plan and our destiny.'*

As disciples, we all face various opportunities to get offended by leadership and other children of God. Still, if we learn to forgive and humble ourselves before God, He will exalt us at the right time. His plan is ultimately to bless us and not to harm us. He is for us and not against us, but as a loving Father, He also disciplines and corrects us when needed.David was willing to go through these times of pause and isolation, tending his Father's sheep, fighting the bear and the lion to protect the sheep from being trained for the calling that was upon his life.

1Samuel 17:34, 35 (TLV) But David said to Saul, *"Your servant has been tending his Father's sheep. When a lion or a bear came and carried off a lamb out of the flock, I went out after it, struck it down, and rescued the lamb out of its mouth. If it rose against me, I grabbed him by its fur, struck it, and killed it."*

How many times do we seek the approval and praise of men? Are you willing to serve God where and when nobody notices? Do you see the battles you are currently facing as stepping stones to the calling God has upon your life?David used his training as a shepherd boy as stepping stones to become a king after God's own heart.

If it wasn't for his pure heart seeking to please the audience of One, I wonder if he would have become king after all. Matthew 6:1 (TPT) says, *"Examine your motives to make sure you're not showing off when you do your good deeds, only to be admired by others; otherwise, you will lose the reward of your heavenly Father."*

In my own life, I've experienced very similar situations in ministry. I started serving in the children's ministry when my children were small and were trained by the Spirit to do everything as if unto the Lord (although it didn't happen overnight), not seeking the recognition of men. I can recall numerous times when I wanted to quit. Still, then the Holy Spirit would come and reward me by unexpectedly manifesting His beautiful presence in our children's church during a Sunday service. While the children's ministry is one of the most unseen, unappreciated ministries in the Body of Christ, God started rewarding me by working in my own children's hearts to serve him individually and wholeheartedly on their own. Today I can surely testify with David - *'Lord, it is clear to me now that how we live will dictate how you deal with us. Good people will taste your goodness, Lord. And to those who are loyal to you, you love to prove that you are loyal and true.'* (Psalm 18:25 (TPT))

Being a parent with grown-up children, I can surely say that the greatest reward does not have a successful public ministry, being influential, or financially prosperous, but seeing my children following in our footsteps in serving God. I encourage every reader that may feel overlooked or misused – stay faithful in serving God. There is a reward! The truth remains – God loves sacrifices.

Although we don't have to bring animal sacrifices anymore as the Israelites did in the Old Testament, we can and ought to still bring our bodies as a living sacrifice unto God. (Romans 12:1,2). When our hearts remain pure, and we serve him because we love bringing our bodies as a living sacrifice to Him, He will give us a harvest of blessings at the right time if we don't get tired of doing good. (Galatians 6:9).

Something exciting I came across when writing this book was the word "selah" written in the book of Psalms. This book was the hymnbook of the Old Testament Jews, and according to famous Bible scholars, most of them were written by King David, while Moses wrote other Moses, Solomon, etc., wrote others.Selah occurs 74 times in the Bible. It occurs seventy-one times in the Psalms and three times in Habakkuk. Although the true meaning of Selah in the Bible is a mystery, many Bible scholars have come up with multiple meanings of the word, that includes: It was a musical notation possibly meaning "silence" or "pause;" others, "end," "a louder strain," "piano," while others think it is similar to a musical interlude, "a pause in the voices singing, while the instruments perform alone." Selah is also translated as "intermission" in the Septuagint (LXX), the earliest Greek translation of the Old Testament.

The writer used 'Selah' to indicate to the reader to pause to reflect on what the Scripture says – think deeply about the meaning of the verse before continuing to read the rest of the passage. Selah. Like David, we all experience seasons when it feels like nothing noteworthy or spectacular happens in our lives as if our lives are on a halt.

David teaches us that these "selah-times" in our lives are seasons in which we should pause, use the intermission to reflect deeply on our relationship with God, and discover who He is. I encourage you to use your time wisely - meditate on his goodness, his faithfulness, and His everlasting love!

Don't be overcome with despair and loneliness; instead, learn to trust and praise Him in these times even more: *'What a glorious God! He gives us salvation over and over, then daily, he carries our burdens! Pause in his presence.* (Psalm 68:20 TPT.) As a full-time pastor serving together with my husband, I've seen many young men and women in the church striving to have a leadership position, but I am not willing to lay down their lives and live sacrificially serving the body of Christ.

God is a jealous God, and He will not share his glory with anyone and therefore, if we aren't willing to humble ourselves before him and fall upon the Rock', He will fall upon us and grind us to powder (Mat 21:44 MKJV)Jesus taught his disciples to wash each other's feet in John 13: 12 – 17 (TPT). *'After washing their feet, he put his robe on and returned to his place at the table. "Do you understand what I just did?" Jesus said. "You've called me your teacher and lord, and you're right, for that's who I am. So if I'm your teacher and lord and have just washed your dirty feet, then you should follow the example that I've set for you and wash one another's dirty feet. Now do for each other what I have just done for you. I speak to you timeless truth: a servant is not superior to his master, and an apostle is never greater than the one who sent him. So now put into practice what I have done for you, and you will experience a life of happiness enriched with untold blessings!'*

If God has given you a dream, be prepared to be trained, tested, and wait for the fulfillment. *'Here's what I've learned through it all: Don't give up; don't be impatient; be entwined as one with the Lord. Be courageous, and never lose hope. Yes, keep on waiting—for he will never disappoint you!* (Psalm 27:14 (TPT))

There is a king (or queen) inside of you waiting to come out, but it will take some purity of heart and motives, perseverance, servanthood, and kindness to make that happen. Remember to continue to grow spiritually in the 'selah' seasons and remain faithful in the little so that God will reward you in the open one day.

May God grant us the heart of David to be able to run the race with courage and obedience and not to be like Jonah, who tried to flee from God's purpose and had to be disciplined to be obedient.

How beautifully the Passion Translation Bible puts Matthew 5:4 - 11 *'What delight comes to you when you wait upon the Lord! For you will find what you long for. What blessing comes to you when gentleness lives in you! For you will inherit the earth. How enriched you are when you crave righteousness! For you will be surrounded with fruitfulness. How satisfied you are when you demonstrate tender mercy! For tender mercy will be demonstrated to you. What bliss you experience when your heart is pure! For then, your eyes will open to see more and more of God. How blessed you are when you make peace! For then, you will be recognized as a true child of God. How enriched you are when you bear the wounds of being persecuted for doing what is right! For that is when you experience the realm of heaven's Kingdom. How ecstatic you can be when people insult and persecute you and speak all kinds of cruel lies about you because of your love for me! So leap for joy—since your heavenly reward is great. For you are being rejected the same way the prophets were before you.'*

Lessons learned from David

1. Willingly submit to authority. This is not a very popular topic, but I found a hundred verses in the Bible that mention submission to authority. One of these is in Hebrews 13:17 (TPT) *'Obey your spiritual leaders and recognize their authority, for they keep watch over your soul without resting since they will have to give an account to God for their work. So it will benefit you when you make their work a pleasure and not a heavy burden.'*

2. Respect and honor the people God has placed over you…even if they can be compared to a "Saul."

3. Stay without offense. Keep your heart pure!

4. Deal with disappointment, especially towards leadership.

5. Be obedient to the call of God, even when serving Him behind the scenes. Regard the tests you go through in these times as stepping stones. God will promote you in the spirit as you pass the test.

QUESTIONS:

Read 1 Samuel 16 – 24 and 1 Kings 1 and 2.

1. In what way were you tested in submission to your leaders in the past?

2. How is David such an excellent example to follow?

3. Evaluate your own life – in what area do you need God to prune still and form your life when comparing yourself to the process in David' life?

CHAPTER 4

Jonah – A Necessary Pause

The book of Jonah tells one of the most popular Bible stories of all time, which records the incident of Jonah being swallowed by a sea-creature – causing a vital pause in his life.

Although many modern scholars argue that the document is mere fiction, Jesus referred to the narrative as natural history (Matthew 12:39-41).

One almost might say that the Lord directed this great pause in Jonah's life to send him to school for three days, and then, strangely enough, the classroom was the belly of a great sea monster. The prophet completed his studies with flying colors and attained a qualification in "mission responsibility"!

This mission all started when God gave Jonah the instruction to go to Nineveh with a message from him. This city was the capital city of Assyria and was a constant threat to Israel. To crown it all, the prophets Hosea and Amos, contemporaries of Jonah, had declared that God would use Assyria to punish his rebellious people, Israel (Hosea 11:5; Amos 5:27). Surely Jonah would be skeptical being a patriotic Israelite - longing for Assyria's destruction! We can just imagine the turmoil in Jonah's mind when he received the Lord's instruction to go to Nineveh.

Although Jonah had to bring a word of judgment to Nineveh, He was aware of the fact that the Lord is a '... *a gracious God, and mer-*

ciful, slow to anger, and of great kindness, and One who repents over calamity.' (Jonah 4:2(b) (MKJV). Hence, it was sure that if the city's inhabitants were to repent after his message, God would undoubtedly spare them. That was the last thing Jonah wanted!

This story confronts us with our inability to love as Jesus does. Just think how you would have reacted would it be you. Still, today God sometimes requires of us things that make us uncomfortable. It could be to show an act of kindness to your enemy, to love the unlovable, to forgive the unforgivable, and show mercy when it is not earned.

On our first mission trip to Zambia, our mission leader led us all to do a prophetic action during our first devotional in which he put a box in the middle of the floor and asked us to climb into the parcel one by one while praying in the spirit until God gave us a heart for the people in the village. It was so profound! You were not allowed to climb out of the box until your heart was moved with compassion for the people we were about to share the Gospel with! Only then were we allowed to start ministering to the unsaved. Maybe Jonah needed an experience like this!

But – Jonah then did what most of us would have done – he fled! He went to Joppa, where he boarded a ship bound for Tarshish, some two thousand miles west. His ultimate goal was to escape from the presence of the Lord (Jonah 1:3).

How many times have you tried to hide from God's presence or fled from his calling upon your life?

Do you also feel the task ahead of you is too difficult to accomplish?

The story continued when a great storm arose, and the crew feared for their very lives. It's then that Jonah confessed that he was the cause of the calamity because of his disobedience. In the beginning, the prophet's sailing companions did not like his suggestion to throw him overboard, but ultimately they were forced to do it to save their own lives, and Jonah ended up sinking into the dark depths of the Mediterranean, seaweed swirling about his head (Jonah 2:5)

It is here that he finally repented, turned back to God, and was vomited on dry land.

Jonah 2:7 – 11 (TLV) *'To the bottoms of the mountains I went down. The earth with her bars was around me, forever! Yet You brought my life up from the Pit, Adonai, my God. As my soul was fading from me, I remembered Adonai, and my prayer came to You, toward Your holy Temple. Those who watch worthless empty things forsake their mercy. But I, with a voice of thanks, will sacrifice to you. What I vowed, I will pay. Salvation is from Adonai." Then Adonai spoke to the fish, and it vomited Jonah onto the dry land.'*

What will it cost to bring you to a place of perfect obedience to God's voice?

John 10:27 (TPT) *'My sheep will hear my voice, and I know each one, and they will follow me.'*

When will you be counted as a mature child of God because of your obedience?

Romans 8:14 (TPT) *'The mature children of God are those who are moved by the impulses of the Holy Spirit.'*

Holy Spirit wants to lead us, yet we are often so stubborn and set in our ways that correction is the only way. Yet God's Word gives us these encouraging promises:

Hebrews 12:5 - 12 (TPT) *'And have you forgotten his encouraging words spoken to you as his children? He said, "My child, don't underestimate the value of the discipline and training of the Lord God, or get depressed when he has to correct you. For the Lord's training of your life is the evidence of his faithful love. And when he draws you to himself, it proves you are his delightful child.'* Fully embrace God's correction as part of your training, for he is doing what any loving father does for his children. For who has ever heard of a child who never had to be corrected? We all should welcome God's discipline as *the validation of authentic sonship. If we have never once endured his correction, it only proves we are strangers and not sons. And isn't it true that we respect our earthly fathers even though they corrected and disciplined us? Then we should demonstrate even greater respect for God, our spiritual Father, as we submit to his life-giving discipline. Our parents corrected us for the short time of our childhood as it seemed good to them. But God corrects us throughout our lives for our good, giving us an invitation to share his holiness. Now all discipline seems to be more pain than pleasure at the time, yet later it will produce a transformation of character, bringing a harvest of righteousness and peace to those who yield to it.'*

Jonah's life ultimately teaches us that pauses or isolation are sometimes exactly what we need to correct us and put us back on track. Although these times don't seem to be something to rejoice about, in the end, it produces everlasting fruit.

James 1:2 – 4 (TPT) *'My fellow believers, when it seems as though you are facing nothing but difficulties, see it as an invaluable opportunity to experience the greatest joy that you can! For you know that when your faith is tested, it stirs up power within you to endure all things. And then as your endurance grows even stronger, it will release perfection into every part of your being until nothing is missing and nothing lacking.'*

Back on his way to Nineveh, a journey estimated to take about more than a month, Jonah had ample time for sober reflection, and he finally entered the city with his short message (consisting of only five words in the Hebrew text):

"*Yet forty days and Nineveh shall be overthrown.*" (Jonah 3:4 (NIV))

To Jonah's amazement, from the king (Asjur-dan III) down to the commoner repented in sackcloth and ashes, and needless to say, but Jonah was agitated and depressed. He found himself on a hilltop nearby, watching the city in anticipation that the Lord would yet destroy it.

The process of disciplining was still incomplete!

It reminds me of the older son in the parable of the prodigal son. He was furious because his Father heartily welcomed back his younger brother after wasting his inheritance in a foreign land.

Luke 15:28 – 30 (TPT) *'The older son became angry and refused to go in and celebrate. So his Father came out and pleaded with him, 'Come and enjoy the feast with us!' "The son said, 'Father, listen! How many years have I been working like a slave for you, performing every duty you've asked as a faithful son? And I've never once disobeyed you. But you've never thrown a party for me because of my faithfulness. Never once have you even given me a goat that I could feast on and celebrate with my friends like he's doing now. But look at this son of yours! He comes back after wasting your wealth on prostitutes and reckless living, and here you are throwing a great feast to celebrate—for him!'*

For us, who's been serving the Lord for many years, there is a warning to take heed to. Don't we sometimes become jealous when God bestows his grace upon the backslidden sinner that disappointed and maybe even misused you when they turn back to God? Often, I've seen sinners returning to God and restored in the church they previously went to only to face hostility from another church member they served with. We need to challenge ourselves concerning this matter and ask the Holy Spirit to pour out his love in our hearts towards the prodigals returning to Jesus.

As Jonah sat in the scorching sun, God caused a vine to grow for shade and comfort, and the prophet rejoiced, but then things turned out to be a disaster once more, and the way the prophet reacted is so typical human.

Jonah 4:7 - 11 (MKJV) But *God prepared a worm as the morning dawned the next day. And it struck the plant, and it withered. And it happened when the sun shone. God ordained a scorching east wind. And the sun beat on the head of Jonah so that he fainted. And he asked for his life to die. And he said Better is my death than my life. And God said to Jonah, is your anger rightly kindled over the plant? And he said, My anger is rightly kindled, even to death. And Jehovah said, You have had pity on the plant, for which you had not labored, nor made it grow, which was a son of a night and perished the son of a night. And should I not spare Nineveh, that great city, in which are more than a hundred and twenty thousand men who do not know between their right and their left hand, besides much cattle?'*

On the following day, however, God sent a worm to smite Jonah's vine, and as the blistering sun beat upon his head, he again lapsed into a state of intense depression.

Then came heaven's stinging rebuke. The Lord in effect said: "Jonah, why is it that you are so concerned with this vine—a mere plant which is temporal, and for which you did not labor; and yet, you utter no concern for the lost inhabitants of Nineveh?"

Aren't most of us more concerned about our comfort than about a dying world that needs to hear the gospel of our Lord Jesus Christ?

How many excuses do we use to justify why we can't be obedient to God's voice in our daily lives?

Lessons learned from Jonah

1. God disciplines His children. '*We all should welcome God's discipline as the validation of authentic sonship. If we have never once endured his correction, it only proves we are strangers and not sons.*' Hebrews 12:8 (TPT)

2. Obedience is a crucial element in our walk with God. It is better than sacrifice 1 Samuel 15:22 says. You can sacrifice your time in prayer and Bible study, but you miss the mark if you are disobedient to the call to make disciples. (In the Hebrew language, the word חטָאָ ("sin") means "to miss." From this, the Hebrew speaker understands that "to sin" means to "miss" the will of God.

3. We need to see the lost through the eyes of Jesus.

4. Gratefulness is one of the most important virtues a child of God should have.

5. God in His supremacy doesn't need our permission to bestow His grace on people.

QUESTIONS:

Read Jonah 1 - 4

1. How obedient will you rate yourself on a scale from 1 – 10?

2. Have you ever run from a responsibility that God has given you? What is/was it all about?

3. What value does discipline play in your Christian walk? How do you usually react when you are corrected or disciplined by a fellow believer or God Himself?

CHAPTER 5

Moses – The Unnecessary Pause

What should have taken the Israelites 11 days eventually took them 40 years to move away from slavery out of Egypt into the Promised Land Canaan! Talk about an unnecessary pause!

In the Books of Exodus and Numbers, we read how God supernaturally delivered the nation of Israel from slavery to the Egyptians.

God promised them a land "flowing with milk and honey," but sadly, they had developed a poverty mindset, deprived of faith due to all their years of slavery.

Needless to say, when Moses sent spies into the land to scout it out, the majority reported that the land was full of strong and mighty warriors. Numbers 13:33 (TLV) *'We also saw there the Nephilim. (The sons of Anak are from the Nephilim.) We seemed like grasshoppers in our eyes as well as theirs!'*

Strangely only two Israeli men (Joshua and Caleb) had the faith to trust God to fulfill his promise; the rest of the men were responsible for the great pause in the desert that was prolonged to 40 years!

We can learn such a lot from these histories' events. One is definitely how our unbelief can hinder us from inheriting God's promise. Secondly is that negativity indeed is the breading place of distrust which would soon prove to be true in the lives of God's chosen people!

While they wandered in the desert, God provided miraculously: manna and quail from heaven for food and water from a rock; yet they kept on complaining and being full of contempt.

Because of their poverty mentality and unbelief, they allowed the enemy to steal from them (John 10:10) when God planned to give them abundantly a "land flowing with milk and honey."

Even today, it remains God's desire for us.

Are you willing to trust that God is the God of the overflow?

Or do you also have a poverty mentality keeping your mind captive?

1 Corinthians 2:9 (TPT) *'This is why the Scriptures say: Things never discovered or heard of before, things beyond our ability to imagine— these are the many things God has in store for all his lovers.'*

We all go through seasons in the wilderness, and often it is a valuable part of our journey, but remember - it is never your final destination!

During these desert times, remember that God will provide for you supernaturally as He met the Israelites needs, but learn to be grateful – don't complain and focus only on the natural as they did! It surely can prolong your journey as in their case! *'And when the people complained, it displeased the LORD: and the LORD heard it; and his anger was kindled; and the fire of the LORD burnt among them, and consumed them that were in the uttermost parts of the camp. And the people cried unto Moses; and when Moses prayed unto the LORD, the fire was quenched. And he called the name of the place Taberah: because the fire of the LORD burnt among them. And the mixt multitude that was among them fell a lusting: and the children of Israel also wept again, and said, Who shall give us flesh to eat? We remember the fish, which we did eat in Egypt freely; the cucumbers, and the melons, and the leeks, and the onions, and the garlic: But now our soul has dried away: there is nothing at all, beside this manna, be-*

fore our eyes.' (Numbers 11:1 – 6 (KJV)

Even after the Lord provided the manna, they complained of not having meat to eat. *"And there went forth a wind from the LORD, and brought quails from the sea, and let them fall by the camp, as it were a day's journey on this side, and as it were a day's journey on the other side, round about the camp, and as it were two cubits high upon the face of the earth. And the people stood up all that day, and all that night, and all the next day, and they gathered the quails: he that gathered least gathered ten homers: and they spread them all abroad for themselves round about the camp. And while the flesh was yet between their teeth, ere it was chewed, the wrath of the LORD was kindled against the people, and the LORD smote the people with a very great plague.'* (Numbers 11:31 – 33 (KJV))

Pay attention to the way God dealt with their discontent and complaining. He gave them their heart's desire (notice the quail fell two cubits high (90 cm), but his wrath was poured out upon them against their greed and gluttony. Could it be that God punished them for their unbelief and distrust? Without faith, it is impossible to please God (Hebrews 11:6). The Word teaches us. The question is – how much did they trust God to provide for all their needs?

Did they truly believe He would look after them?

And today – how much do you trust Him to provide in your needs?

Do we honestly believe Philippians 4:19 (KJV) *'But my God shall supply all your need according to his riches in glory by Christ Jesus'* or do we question his character when we go through desert times?

Your wilderness experience doesn't have to last 40 years, 40 weeks, or even 40 days. What we genuinely need is unwavering trust, faith, and perseverance to inherit our promised land! We need to learn to trust God in the wilderness (even if our journey is prolonged), or we'll never reach our destination!

The saddest part of this story is that Moses never had the privilege to enter the promised land. The reason why Moses wasn't permitted; is given in Deuteronomy 32:51–52 (MKJV) *'because you sinned against Me among the sons of Israel at the Waters of Strife in Kadesh, in the wilderness of Zin, because you did not sanctify Me amid the sons of Israel. Yet you shall see the land before you, but you shall not go there to the land which I am giving to the sons of Israel.'* God fulfilled his promise by showing Moses the Promised Land, but he was not allowed to enter.

In Numbers 20, we read how the Israelites came to the Desert of Zin at the end of their forty years of wandering, desperately in need of water, once more complaining against Moses and Aaron. After enquiring from God, He told Moses and Aaron to gather the Israelites and speak to the rock and water that will come forth. Moses did as he was commanded but then instead of speaking to the rock, he, seemingly in anger and frustration, struck the rock twice with his staff (Numbers 20:10,11). The water was released from the rock, but God reprimanded Moses and Aaron that, because they failed to trust Him enough to honor Him as holy, they would not bring the children of Israel into the Promised Land (verse 12).

How many times have you acted out in anger and frustration?

How many times have you lost your temper when working with rebellious people? Yet, God still shows mercy to us!

The punishment Moses received may seem harsh to us, but when examining his actions, we see a few mistakes we can learn from. Firstly, Moses was disobedient to God's direct command when he was told to speak to the rock but struck it instead. Even though God instructed him to hit the rock earlier in their journey (Exodus 17), His instructions differ here. Trust is a high value to God, and He again wanted Moses to trust him. After all, they were in such a close relationship throughout their journey. Moses had to obey God and trust that He would be true to his promise.

We all fail in this area of our walk with God.

How many times have you questioned God's methods and try to do it your way?

How many times do we fall back in our old ways of doing things when God wants to do something new in our lives?

How obedient are you to the voice of your shepherd? Joh 10:14 – 16 (TPT) *"I alone am the Good Shepherd, and I know those whose hearts are mine, for they recognize me and know me, just as my Father knows my heart and I know my Father's heart. I am ready to give my life to the sheep. "And I have other sheep that I will gather which are not of this Jewish flock. And I, their shepherd, must lead them too, and they will follow me and listen to my voice. And I will join them all into one flock with one shepherd.'*

Then, Moses seemed to take the credit for themselves for the miracle when he said: *"Listen, you rebels, must **we** bring you water out of this rock?"* (Numbers 20:10 (NIV), emphasis added). Because Moses said this to the whole nation, God did not let this go unpunished but wanted the Israelites to respect His holiness.

What a warning to us as well! It is so easy to take credit for our gifts and receive the praise of men. The best we can do is always give praise back to God (the Giver of all gifts) instead of getting puffed up and set ourselves up for a fall.

When we look a little deeper at the symbolism, we see the rock symbolized Christ in 1 Corinthians 10:4. Christ was crucified once (Hebrews 7:27) just as the stone was struck in Exodus 17:6. Moses' speaking to the rock in Numbers 20 portrays our prayer life. We only need to pray in faith to Jesus Christ that was "struck" for our sins to provide us living water continuously! Moses, therefore, destroyed the Biblical typology and, in effect, crucified Christ again.

What does your prayer life look like?

How intimate is your walk with God?

How much do we trust God to have his way?

How many times do we take matters into our own hands?

God's punishment was severe. Moses was deprived of entering the Promised Land (Numbers 20:12), yet Moses accepted God's judgment and continued to lead God's people faithfully and honor him.

What an example of godliness! It is so easy to get angry with God when you are corrected or punished. Yet, God's Word calls us true sons when we are disciplined. Hebrew 12:9 (TPT) *'And isn't it true that we respect our earthly fathers even though they corrected and disciplined us? Then we should demonstrate even greater respect for God, our spiritual Father, as we submit to his life-giving discipline.'*

The story ends with a beautiful display of God's compassion to Moses when He invited Moses to Mount Nebo and showed him the Promised Land before his death. *'And Jehovah said to him, 'this is the land which I swore to Abraham, to Isaac, and Jacob, saying, I will give it to your seed. I have caused you to see it with your eyes, but you shall not go over there.'* Deuteronomy 34:4-5 (MKJV)

Moses' pause in the desert ended in a detrimental pause when he died there in Moab. Yet this mistake did not disqualify him being a true friend of God. God continued to love him with tenderness, and it is stated in Deuteronomy 34:5-6 (NIV) that God buried Moses himself – *'And Moses, the servant of the Lord, died there in Moab, as the Lord has said. He buried him in Moab, in the valley opposite Beth Peor, but to this day, no one knows where his grave is.'*

Lessons learned from Moses:

1. God uses the seemingly unequipped to fulfill a great call. Remember, Moses complained that he couldn't speak properly. 'Moses said to the LORD, "*Pardon your servant, Lord. I have never been eloquent, neither in the past nor since you have spoken to your servant. I am slow of speech and tongue.*" Exodus 4:10 (NIV). Remember, God then gave him Aaron to assist him.

2. Complaining can disqualify you from entering your destiny.

3. God's wrath upon the disobedient is real. Romans 1:18 (NIV) "*For the wrath of God is revealed from heaven against all ungodliness and unrighteousness of men, who by their unrighteousness suppress the truth.*"

4. God honors his leaders and gives them enough grace to fulfill the call he placed upon them.

5. God is a compassionate God – His mercy is new every morning. This is what is revealed to us at the end of Moses's life: Lamentations 3:22-24 (NKJV) '*Through the Lord's mercies we are not consumed, because His compassions fail not. They are new every morning; Great is Your faithfulness. "The Lord is my portion," says my soul, "Therefore I hope in Him!"*

QUESTIONS

Read Exodus 1 – 40 and Numbers 1 - 22

1. How do we disqualify ourselves on our journey to our destiny?

2. What is your contribution to advancing on your journey?

3. What lesson do you learn out of Moses's life that can enrich your own?

CHAPTER 6

Esther – The Purposeful Pause

If you read the book of Esther, you almost get the feeling that God pressed the pause button in His Word and left for a while. It's almost as if He took leave or went on a Sabbatical because it is the only Bible book that does not mention God even once. It feels very significant because it portrays moments in history and even in our own lives when God does not seem anywhere to be found, almost as if He is absent.

It also reveals how people live without acknowledging God in their lives.To be honest - most of us experience seasons where God feels distant, and then we are faced with the question - how do you live in these times when God doesn't seem near?
Most of us know the story.

Esther underwent a full year of preparation (Esther 2:12) before she was chosen to be queen. As an orphan girl, she laid herself down and became obedient to her uncle's proposal to adopt her as his own. For the first six months, she was soaked in the oil of myrrh (Esther 2:12). Talk of a luxurious yet sacrificial pause in her life! The same anointing oil used to anoint the high priest (Exodus 30:22-31; see also Psalm 133). Oil is a symbol of the Holy Spirit, and myrrh is associated with the death and burial of Jesus (Mark 15:23; John 19:39). It reminds us of the life of a true believer when we repent, die to our sins, get born again, and go through a season where the Holy Spirit starts regenerating us.

We get baptized (identifying ourselves with the death and resurrection of Christ), and baptized in the Holy Spirit, and start walking in the anointing upon our lives. These events are the most crucial in the life of a believer.

When we get born again, it is almost as if God stops us in our tracks, and a new life in Christ begins. We then grow through the processes mentioned above that form the foundation stones on which our faith is built as we start a new life in Christ. (See Hebrews 6:1-3)

Esther's year of preparation also symbolizes the Bride of Christ (the true church) that is currently busy preparing and getting ready for the Wedding of the Lamb, Jesus Christ:

'For the wedding of the Lamb has come, and his bride has made herself ready. Fine linen, bright and clean, was given her to wear. (Fine linen stands for the righteous acts of the saints.).' (Revelation 19:7 (NIV))
"I saw the Holy City, the new Jerusalem, coming down out of heaven from God, prepared as a bride beautifully dressed for her husband." (Revelation 21:2 (NIV))
It also symbolizes an essential attribute of the true church that does only what God's Word tells her to do. As children of God, we must learn to follow the guidance of the Holy Spirit and to do His will, to submit and obey, without rebellion or disobedience.

A helpful lesson we learn from these above events in isolation is to remain faithful and constant even when you're all alone, when it seems heavens are brass and God is silent. When the "music fades, and all is stripped away…go back to the heart of worship," the old worship song said. In those moments where God seems most absent, God works behind the scenes where we cannot see! We need only to trust God. We don't have to understand everything! Just because you don't see the sun in your garage doesn't mean the sun is not shining!

It may feel that you are constantly swimming upstream in these lonely times, and it is easy to slack down or change your direction to a more comfortable downstream slide. Esther's life encourages us to remain faithful to a calling even if we feel forgotten and as if the resistance is too stiff.

Again, like so many times in his Word, we see how He uses the most unlikely people to do the most peculiar work in his powerful plan of redemption!

Like most true stories, there is always a scoundrel in the story, too.

In the book of Esther, it is the vengeful, cruel advisor to the king, Haman. He detested Mordecai after he refused to bow down to him, and therefore he plotted to wipe out the entire Jewish nation.

Haman said to the king, *'There is a certain people scattered abroad and dispersed among the peoples in all the provinces of your kingdom whose customs are different from those of all other people and who do not obey the king's laws; it is not in the king's best interest to tolerate them.'* (Esther 3:8 NIV). What happened next caused a significant threat to God's people as the king gave him the authority to decide the Jewish people's future. Haman immediately announced a government-issued edict of genocide.

In every child of God's life, there is a necessary preparation period in which your character is formed, and you go through many tests of obedience, submission, and endurance. And in Esther's life, it was no different! For a whole month, the king had not requested her presence, and her life was in danger should she come to him without his permission (according to Persian customs of that time.) Mordecai then reminded her of her divine purpose as queen and that silence wasn't an option. Est 4:13,14 (TLV) Mordecai *told them to reply to Esther with this answer, "Do not think in your soul that you will escape in the king's household more than all the Jews. For if you remain silent at this time, relief and deliverance will arise for the Jews from another place—but you and your father's house will perish. Who knows whether you have attained a royal status for such a time as this?"*

So, the entire Jewish nation was brought to a pause! Ester called them to a 3-day fast before she made a life-or-death decision. She knew that going to the king unsummoned could lead to her death sentence because anyone who came into the king's presence uninvited could be executed. Indeed, her bravery and obedience confront our timid behavior and challenge us to be obedient no matter what the cost!

Esther stepped out in faith; after the fast, she dressed in her best royal robes, approached the king, and revealed Haman's plot against her people. The events took a surprising turn when the Jewish people were saved, and Haman hung on the gallows he had prepared for Mordecai, and to crown it all, Esther received Haman's estate.

Even though God is never mentioned in this book, there are precious lessons we can successfully apply to our lives.

God will finish the good work He has started in us! God has no favorites (Acts 10:34) and will complete his purpose in our lives. He never withdraws the gifts and the calling He placed upon our lives. We just need to be obedient and walk in that calling and purpose He has for us!

Philippians 1:6 (TPT) *'I pray with great faith for you, because I'm fully convinced that the One who began this glorious work in you will faithfully continue the process of maturing you and will put his finishing touches to it. Until the unveiling of our Lord Jesus Christ!'*

Romans 11:29 (TLV) for *the gifts and the calling of God are irrevocable.*

God used Esther with her beauty and bravery to deliver the people he loved so much. She was placed in the palace to bring deliverance to the Jewish nation and fulfill God's divine plan for her life, and so He will do in your life if you only believe!

We are called to make a difference! Your life counts! You can change circumstances drastically through your obedience.

The life of Esther is very dear to me personally. Years back, I was still teaching and teaching at a Christian school with a heart for the poor. (Many of the children were funded by the school that is situated in an underprivileged area.)

As I started at the new school, I was woken by the Spirit at 3 o'clock one morning in the first week. I felt led to read the book of Esther, and as I went to my prayer room and started reading, the Spirit spoke to me. He revealed that the Christian school I was part of; was in desperate need of finances.

He continued to show me what we should do to get a breakthrough. I started writing down the prophetic word the Spirit gave me, and the same morning I went to the school's pastor and submitted the comment. He received the word with a receptive heart and called out a fast of three days. The principal and the pastor were obedient to what was revealed by the Spirit, and after the three days fast, they went to the government offices to apply for a bursary. The favor of the Lord was upon the meeting, and their request was met. They received enough funds to pay their debt and pay for the new learning material for the rest of the year needed to continue serving the poor.

God is faithful to his promises. He honored the leadership and the staff's obedience, fasting, and prayer and came to our rescue!

Proverbs 19:17 (TPT) *'Every time you give to the poor, you make a loan to the Lord. Don't worry—you'll be repaid in full for all the good you've done.'*

Obedience remains the key to prayers getting answered!

As believers, we need to take up our responsibility when God speaks to us. You may just be the answer to the prayer, and God will use you if you are willing – otherwise, he will find someone else. The best thing we can do is to search for and surrender to his divine purpose for our lives!

> **Lessons learned from Esther**:
>
> 1. Prayer and fasting is God's secret weapon. The benefits of fasting and prayer are the best discussed in Isaiah 58 (NIV). It will bring deliverance and freedom (it will "*untie the cords of the yoke*" and "*set the oppressed free*" (v. 6). It continues to say that "*light will break forth like the dawn*" and "*your healing will quickly appear*" (v. 8). Most of all, your relationship with the Lord will become more intimate, and you will be able to hear God's voice when you cry to Him for help (v. 9). Then there are promises of God's guidance, provision, and strength; you will become "*like a well-watered garden; like a spring whose waters never fail*" (v. 11). When you are suffering from depression, joy will flow over you instead (v. 14). All this through prayer and fasting!
>
> 2. Corporate prayer and fasting can save a nation from destruction and the wicked plans of the enemy confused and overthrown, as proven in the book of Esther.
>
> 3. God is no respecter of a person! He doesn't call the equipped; He equips those He calls.
>
> 4. The nation of Israel is God's chosen people, and those who oppose Israel will be God's enemies. Zechariah 12: 8,9 (NIV) '*On that day the Lord will shield those who live in Jerusalem, so that the feeblest among them will be like David, and the house of David will be like God, like the Angel of the Lord going before them. On that day, I will set out to destroy all the nations that attack Jerusalem.*'

5. We become part of God's chosen nation through our faith in Jesus. The Bible uses the imagery of an olive tree. Those who are not born Jewish (the wild olive branch) but came to faith in Jesus are grafted into the real, cultivated olive tree to become a joint partner who shares the beautiful richness of the cultivated olive stem. Romans 11 tell all about this beautiful inheritance we attain through our faith in Jesus. Rom 11:17, 18 (TPT) *'However, some of the branches have been pruned away. And you, who were once nothing more than a wild olive branch in the desert, God has grafted in—inserting you among the remaining branches as a joint partner to share in the wonderful richness of the cultivated olive stem. So don't be so arrogant as to believe that you are superior to the natural branches. There's no reason to boast, for the new branches don't support the root, but you owe your life to the root that supports you!'*

QUESTIONS:

Read Esther 1 - 10

1. What value did the story of Esther add to your walk with God?

2. In what area in your life do you need a breakthrough? How can you apply these truths to accomplish the required breakthrough?

3. How can you take up greater responsibility for your life?

CHAPTER 7

Paul – The Worthwhile Pause

Saul of Tarsus, who became Paul after his conversion on the road to Damascus, is known as one of the most influential leaders of the first generation of Christians and the founder of Christianity.
28 percent of the New Testament was written the Apostle Paul, which includes thirteen books. Still, his writings are also the most quoted in the Bible.

Interestingly, when counting the number of words, Luke the physician and historian contributed more stories in the New Testament, which amounts to 37,932 words. Paul then comes in second at 32,408, yet today the average Christian sermon uses more quotations from Paul's writings.

What made Paul's writings so famous and still so relevant for the time we live in?

Maybe it is because we can relate to Paul's pre-Christ and post-Christ journey. Most readers can testify that their lives changed radically after encountering the living God and getting born again. Our thirst for righteousness and the hunger for the will of God (like in the life of Paul) is the proof of genuine salvation!

Paul went through an extreme life-changing pause that determined the cause of his life. He was on his way to Damascus when a bright light shuns from heaven, and a voice confronted him '... *"Saul, Saul, why are you persecuting Me?"* (Acts 9:4 (b) (TLV). Though this is the version we find in the book of Acts, we read in Corinthians that Paul said that he saw the Lord (1 Corinthians 9:1). Galatians 1:16 states that God revealed his Son to him. Galatians 1:16 – 18 (TPT) then describes an even greater pause after Paul's conversion: *'God's grace unveiled his Son in me so that I would proclaim him to the non-Jewish people of the world. After this encounter, I kept it a secret for some time, sharing it with no one. And I chose not to run to Jerusalem to try to impress those who had become apostles before me. Instead, I went away into the Arabian Desert for a season until I returned to Damascus, where I had first encountered Jesus. I remained there for three years until I eventually went up to Jerusalem and met the apostle Peter and stayed with him for a couple of weeks so I could get to know him better.'*

The question is – What happened in those three years of isolation in the Arabian Desert, and how can this information enhance our walk with God?

Warren Wiersbe's research (an American Christian Bible teacher and commentator, conference speaker, and prolific writer of Christian literature and theological works) states that during those three years, "Paul gave himself to study, prayer, and meditation, and met with the Lord alone." Many other Bible teachers believe that this was Paul's three years with the Lord, just as the other apostles physically had spent three years with Christ while He was together with them on earth.

When we look at our walk with God, we realize that it starts with the conversion, but it doesn't end there. It is only the beginning. We get a hunger for God's Word, and spending time in the Word enables us to grow spiritually. 1Peter 2:2 (TPT) *'In the same way that nursing infants cry for milk, you must intensely crave the pure spiritual milk of God's Word. This "milk" will cause you to grow into maturity, thoroughly nourished and strong for life— '.* Just as babies need regular feeding times, like newborn children, we also need to set time apart in our day to meet with God.

Interestingly, after Paul's time in the desert, he emerged prepared to communicate divine truth revealed to him on his mission trips. It's also in our own quiet time with the Lord where we learn to hear His voice and where He reveals life-changing revelations in His Word.

Through His Holy Spirit, the Lord Jesus wants to disciple us in these precious times alone with Him. I urge you to get a private place where you can daily meet with the Lord. Many years back, when my children were toddlers, till my husband and I gave our lives to the Lord, I had this immense hunger to know Him more. I'm sure many mothers will be able to relate with me when I say that time alone is a luxury when your children are that small!

I desperately longed to spend time with this newfound Lover of my soul named Jesus. During that time, I asked the Lord to provide me with a Wendy hut to pray and study God's Word. I'll never forget the day I received a refund on my tax and was able to buy my little wooden house of prayer. It became my war room!

Most mornings, I woke up early before the children were up and met my Saviour in my hut. I particularly remember early one summer morning when I opened the door; I saw a cloud of glory in my spirit as I entered the room. Holy Spirit was waiting to meet me there.

From there on, it became the secret place where I poured out my heart before the Father; a place where He shared His secrets with me; a place where I warred for family and friends salvation and even for nations to come to the Lord. It became the most precious time of my day, and when we went away on holiday, I often longed to be back at our secret place.

I encourage you to have a regular meeting place where you can set time apart for God. I've heard many people say they don't have times like these because God is omnipresent, and they talk with Him wherever they are...which, of course, is true. Still, I've often said to those people: "In a marriage, there are intimate times with your spouse where no one else is present, it's a place where you get to know one another on the deepest level of intimacy, and often impregnation takes place. There is a parallel in the spirit.

God longs for these intimate times. He is a Rewarder for those who diligently seek Him. During these intimate times, He impregnates us with His Word, where the logos word becomes rhema. (Both logos and rhema are the Word of God, but the former is God's Word objectively recorded in the Bible, while the latter is the word of God spoken to us at a specific occasion.)

Another critical thing to mention is that you receive a commission that generally has to do with people every time you encounter God.

Paul's life is such an example of transformation! Before his conversion, he persecuted the Christians, thinking that He did God a favor, but he began his ministry after three years in the desert.

Everything he previously thought he knew about God had to be re-evaluated in the light of the new revelation he got from spending time with God. This is precisely what needs to happen with a newborn child of God. We need to be transformed into the image of Jesus, and the more time we spend with him, the more we are changed.

2Corinthians 5:17 (TLV) *'Therefore, he is a new creation if anyone is in Messiah. The old things have passed away; behold, all things have become new.'*

As a Pharisee, Paul knew Scripture very well, but the truth that Jesus was the promised Messiah shook the foundation he'd been trusting.

How many of our foundations were shaken after our conversion?

Many times we only view the Father as this distant, angry God that just waits to punish us for doing wrong. We don't think that we can have a personal relationship with Him and that He can be trusted with the finest detail of our lives.

This is due to a religious mindset that hinders us from experiencing an intimate walk with the Holy Spirit. Discipleship is very valuable in dealing with issues such as this. Sometimes we just need someone to come alongside us and mentor us in the ways of God.

Paul was a disciple-maker. He took Timothy under his wing: *'Timothy, you are my true spiritual son in the faith. May abundant grace, mercy, and total well-being from God the Father and the Anointed One, our Lord Jesus, be yours!'* (1 Timothy 1:2 (TPT)); often referred to him as his *'son,'* a *'beloved brother and co-worker'* (1 Thessalonians 3:2(TPT)); and deposited many truths into his life *'So, my son Timothy, don't forget all that has been deposited within you. Escape from the empty echoes of men and the perversion of twisted reasoning'*. (1 Timothy 6:20(TPT))

Disciple-making is the Biblical pattern Jesus modeled in the New Testament.

Just PAUSE; quietly and deeply think about this!

We read in the Gospels how He called the disciples one by one and walked, stayed, and ministered with them for three years. He modeled what He taught them. Paul walked in His footsteps even though he didn't have the privilege the other twelve disciples had of physically having Him with them. Yet, he had the Holy Spirit, we also have today, that enables us to walk an even closer walk!

Paul motivated his disciples to follow in his footsteps as a dedicated mentor would: *'My beloved friends, imitate my walk with God and follow all those who walk according to the way of life we modeled before you.'* Philippians 3:17 (TPT)

This is the blueprint God has for His church: "*Now go in my authority and make disciples of all nations, baptizing them in the name of the Father, the Son, and the Holy Spirit. And teach them to follow all that I have commanded you faithfully. And never forget that I am with you every day, even to the completion of this age.*" (Matthew 28:

19,20 (TPT))

Disciple-making is about covenant relationships. Ruth spoke about this kind of relationship when her mother-in-law urged her to go back to her nation of birth, and she said: '... *Do not beg me to leave you to return from following after you.*

For where you go, I will go. Where you stay, I will stay. Your people shall be my people, and your God my God. Where you die, I will die, and there I will be buried. May Jehovah does so to me, and more also, if anything but death parts you and me.' Ruth 1: 16 (b),17 (MKJV) Ruth knew something about covenant relationships. Her mother-in-law was left a widow when her husband passed away. She lost her two sons and had no means to look after her two daughters-in-law. She could not offer them anything, yet Ruth decided to stay with her, and most of us know the outcome of the story.

In short, Boaz, being near to kin to the deceased and the nearest of all now alive, married Ruth, and therefore, she became the great, great grandmother of Jesus! May this encourage us to honor covenant relationships that come through disciple-making. John 15: 12,13 (NIV) *'This is My commandment, that you love one another as I have loved you. Greater love has no one than this that he lay down his life for his friends.'*

Long after Paul left the desert and began his ministry, the Lord kept working in and through him. The transformation that took place in the years spent in the desert of Arabia had a detrimental effect on his ministry, and from there, on forwarding, he kept growing to be more and more like Jesus.

Above all, he valued disciple-making and mentoring relationships highly.

Interesting to note that Paul had three close discipleship relationships – Barabas, Silas, and Timothy. While Jesus had Peter, James, and John in his inner circle. . We can receive such a lot of truths from each of these relationships Paul had.

BARNABAS – THE OLDER MAN, THE MENTOR RELATIONSHIP

Barnabas was a much-matured believer and one of the first people God brought into his life as a new believer. You will recall that Paul previously vehemently opposed the Christians, and the church in Jerusalem was understandably skeptical. Still, Barnabas bridged the gap and built relationships with Paul himself and between Paul and the church family. He began to disciple and be a mentor for Paul. We all know how valuable a relationship like this can be and greatly value the younger believer's growth.

In Acts 11, when Barnabas found a growing group of believers in Antioch who needed shepherding and a church planted for their support and ministry, Barnabas believed Paul would assist. He invited Paul to come and help in this church planting ministry.

Every disciple of the Lord, mostly the young, needs a mentor in life. These mentors usually are a bit older in years and experience and are a rich resource of knowledge, skill, and wisdom. Young believers are generally full of energy and zeal, but nothing can replace the years of experience. In Acts 13, we see God calling them to do mission work together as a duo in the regions beyond, reproducing what God had done in Antioch.

SILAS – THE PEER, MUTUAL DISCIPLE RELATIONSHIP

Shortly after Paul and Barnabas were back in Antioch reporting about their mission trip to the church (Acts 15), they were sent to Jerusalem to discuss several Jewish believers who had come to Antioch and caused some confusion Gentile believers there.

After they addressed and settled these concerns, the church in Jerusalem sent a letter of clarification from the churches' side and sent two respected leaders to represent the church family and affirm their position and attitude toward the Gentile brothers in Christ. Silas was one of those men.

He stayed behind in Antioch while his traveling companion returned to Jerusalem. We read at the end of chapter 15 how Paul and Silas became acquainted with one another and went on a mission trip together.From there on, Paul and Silas co-labored in the mission field and became covenant disciples. They faced a lot of trials and tribulations together. When they came to Philippi, Paul cast a demon out of a female fortune-teller, ruining her income and popularity.

Because of that, Paul and Silas were severely beaten and thrown into prison, their feet bound in stocks. What happened in the middle of the night; is proof of their mutual faith and companionship.

They started praying and singing hymns to God until an earthquake forced the doors open, and everyone's chains fell off. Paul and Silas boldly stood up and proclaimed the gospel, converting the terrified jailer. It didn't end there; they explained the gospel to the others in his house, and that evening his entire household got saved and was baptized. When the magistrates found out that Paul and Silas were Roman citizens, the rulers felt guilty because of how they treated them and apologized and let the two men go. (Acts 16:25 – 40). Later on, in their lives, Paul and Silas stayed friends and continue to do mission work in Thessalonica, Berea, and Corinth.

God made us relational beings. Just like the God-head (three in one – God, the Father, Jesus, His Son, and Holy Spirit) are in a close, intimate relationship with one another, we are also made to form such godly relationships.

We need to surround ourselves with people that we can share our dreams with, someone that you feel comfortable to share your heart with, someone that will not judge you but will listen and encourage you to follow the right path, someone that will celebrate your victories but will also lend an ear and a shoulder in troubled times.

The key to healthy discipleship-friendships is built on mutual trust, respect, and honesty. I believe people are tired of what I call "plastic" relationships built on fear and pretense.

TIMOTHY – A RELATIONSHIP WHERE YOU DISCIPLE THE YOUNG

Timothy was still a young man, but his church family had so much respect for him, and Paul saw his God-given potential and started investing in him. Paul included Timothy in his traveling ministry team, and later on, he served in churches planted by this team.

We see that Paul duplicated what he experienced when Barnabas believed in him as a young convert and allowed him to minister with him in the mission field when everyone doubted his character. Paul, in his turn, took Timothy under his wing and mentored him throughout his life.

We need to invest in the younger generation because if we don't, we'll die with the baton in our hands with nobody to carry the legacy we've travailed for.

Paul and Timothy's discipleship-relationship stages teach us valuable lessons we can follow to be more effective in serving God.

Stage One: Parenthood (Teach)

Right from the beginning of their relationship, we find that Paul fulfilled Timothy's role as a spiritual father. Paul addresses him as *"my true spiritual son in the faith."* (1 Timothy 1:2 (TPT). Timothy's biological father was Greek, and we find no evidence that he was a Christian. Indeed, this must have meant the world to the young man. When Paul was on his way to his second mission trip, he stops at Lystra to pick up Timothy. This young disciple would accompany him and serve as sort of an apprentice under him. (Acts 16)

If we look at the world we live in, we find a generation without fathers. Over 60% of South African kids are in homes without fathers. Ten percent of these households have lost the father due to death, and 50% are alive but are not present in their kids' lives. (These stats were acquired from the Stats SA General Household Survey 2016/2017.) According to the U.S. Census Bureau, 19.7 million children, more than 1 in 4, live without a father in the home. (2017. U.S. Census Bureau.)

The church faces a severe challenge when faced with making disciples of the next generation!

Stage Two: Balancing (Model)
The second stage of disciple-making is modeling how to balance your spiritual life with your personal life. Paul's second letter to Timothy points out that he should be followed – *'You, however, closely followed my teaching, manner of life, purpose, faithfulness, patience, love, perseverance—'* (2 Timothy 3:10-11 (TLV)). Paul sets the example of doing life and handling challenges and asks Timothy to imitate him as he imitates Christ. The next generation is always watching, so we get to set the pace by making disciples wherever we are.

Stage Three: Co-labouring (Re-produce)

In the book of Romans, we find this exciting reference that Paul makes to Timothy in chapter 16, verse 21 (TPT), *'My ministry partner, Timothy, sends his loving greetings, …'*. We sense the growth that has taken place in Timothy's spiritual life as he has gone from being a son to a student and now to be a partner and a co-laborer.

Maybe we should change the time we invest in praying for the laborers of the harvest and start investing more time in those disciples with the potential to become our co-laborers in the mission.

PAUSE AND THINK ABOUT THIS – You are reading this because God urges you to take up the responsibility to disciple someone. Ask the Holy Spirit to show you who it is. The baton has been passed on to you! Are you willing to invest your time and knowledge into these three stages to enhance the Kingdom of God and leave a legacy behind? God wants us to partner with Him until Jesus comes!

Lessons learned from Paul

1. Disciple relationships should be mutually building and sharpening as stated in Proverbs 27:17 (TLV) *'Iron sharpens iron; so a man sharpens the countenance of his friend.'* We can learn a lot in the way Paul mentored Timothy, consistently communicating his admiration, respect, and gratitude for him as a fellow worker in the kingdom of God.

2. The church faces a severe challenge when faced with making disciples of the next generation!

3. God did not create us to live for ourselves without any meaningful relationships with others. Remember, God is a relational God, and we need to walk in His footsteps if we want to live close to Him.

4. We will be accountable to the Lord for the stewardship of our relationships. Be trustworthy, loving, and honest.

5. Create an atmosphere where people will not feel judged but loved irrespective of their moral failure at times. Remember – we are all still on this journey to become more like Christ, and none has arrived yet.

6. Leave a spiritual legacy behind; don't pass away one day with the baton still in your hand.

QUESTIONS:

Read Acts 1 – 28

1. What new revelations did you get concerning disciple-making?

2. Name a few challenges we face when making disciples.

3. Discuss the benefits of making disciples.

CHAPTER 8

Jesus - The Controversial Pause

If you feel as if somebody pressed the pause button on your life, you are in good company. Jesus had to wait 30 years before he was released to fulfill His call and ministry. Then, for three years, acceleration took place. His church was jam-packed; then, he was crucified on a cross to die for the human race, thereby fulfilling His mission of providing a way out of sin and death. We learn that even Jesus had to wait for the appointed time God the Father had in mind.

As humans that live in an instant society where we have instant coffee, microwave ovens, the internet, online shopping, waiting for God's breakthrough can seem like an eternity. You may feel that you are forgotten and as if the breakthrough is never coming. Many times we start questioning God's character or doubt if we even heard the Lord correctly.

Some turn their backs on God and lose their faith, but I want to encourage you to keep your eyes on our compassionate, loving Jesus, who came to earth to become the Son of man. He became man so that He could identify with us. He was tested and went through every trial and tribulation you would ever go through. Therefore He always pauses at our weaknesses and failures and strengthens and uplifts us when we spend time in His presence.
Isaiah 40:31 (TLV), *but they who wait for Adonai will renew their*

strength. They will soar up with wings as eagles. They will run and not grow weary. They will walk and not be faint.

It is precisely what Jesus very often did – He paused. He paused whenever He was moved with compassion – to strengthen the weak, heal the sick, raise the dead, deliver the demonic oppressed or demonstrate His love and salvation to a sinner.

Still today – God pauses when we need Him to pause. He pauses to help.

The story of the Samaritan woman in John 4 describes such a helpful, compassionate pause. Joh 4:3,4 (TLV) *'So He left Judea and went back again to the Galilee. But He needed to pass through Samaria.'* He was scheduled to announce the Kingdom of God among the Jews, and that mission did not include a side trip in Samaria. However, He met a receptive woman who was hungry for the truth and ready to receive the gift of salvation.

At that time, there was tremendous animosity between Jews and Samaritans because they were descendants of the intermarrying of Jews and the ancient Assyrians.

Thus, the Jews hated them for making the race impure. *'Then the Samaritan woman tells Him, "How is it that You, a Jew, ask me, a Samaritan woman, for a drink?" (For Jewish people don't deal with Samaritans.)'* (John 4:9 (TLV)) Just to recap, Jesus, paused along the way to Galilee and approached a Samaritan woman for water as she came to fetch water for herself at the well. He then told her God wanted to give her a gift, a gift of living water that would give eternal life. We read how Jesus met her where she was. He paused on his predestined journey for an outcast who was caught up in deep emotional distress and who was in desperate need of salvation.

That is the God we serve - He meets us in our plain, everyday, mundane places of need. There He acknowledges the pains and disappointments we struggle with and brings living water to those thirsty places. God pauses so that we can experience Him if only we would be willing to believe there is something more than what our eyes see.

Not only does God pause at our disappointments, but He also pauses to appoint each one of His disciples; that includes you and me as well.

Just pause and think of how Jesus' disciples had to deal with His death. They had spent three years living and ministering with their Messiah. They shared their hearts with Him, broke bread together, and saw many miracles taken place, just to come to a place where Jesus was taken from them.
All their dreams of a future together were shattered at Golgotha. Suddenly their joy was replaced with fear and uncertainty. Imagine the sense of despair and hopelessness when He was buried in a tomb and the silence came with the loss of a precious loved one.

If you have ever attended a musical concert, you may have experienced exactly this. Suddenly there is a silence when the composition seems to end. Assuming it is the conclusion, the audience begins to applaud, only to hear the musicians starting the same piece's next movement. This is called a grand pause. It is not the end of the musical composition but rather a distinct break between selections. The musicians guide the audience from ending one piece to the beginning of another.

The devil thought he defeated Jesus and Christianity, but little did he know that this was only a grand pause for him to be resurrected and the Church to be birthed! The pause had to take place so that Jesus could be hidden in the grave for three days for Him to descend into hell, take back the keys of death from Satan and ascend back into heaven to prepare a place for us. (Acts 1:9; Ephesians 4:9,10; Acts 2:31; 1 Peter 4:6; I Corinthians 15:26; Revelations 1:18)
Revelation 1:18 (TPT) *'the Living One! I was dead but now look—I am alive forever and ever. And I hold the keys that unlock death and the*

unseen world.'

Jesus won the battle and triumphed as the Lion of the Tribe of Juda, who still saves His children against the enemy!

Today we have the keys, symbolic of the authority children of God have.

Matthew 16:19 (TPT) *I will give you the keys of heaven's kingdom realm to forbid on earth that which is forbidden in heaven, and to release on earth that which is released in heaven."*

If you go through times of pause and you are getting weary and discouraged while waiting upon the promises of God, remind yourself that this is not the end. It is just the 'selah' moment until a new season in your life starts. God is about to do something new! It is about to be birthed!

Isaiah 42:9 (TLV) *Behold, the former things have come to pass, Now I declare new things. Before they spring forth, I announce them to you."*

Isaiah 43:19 (TLV) *Here I am, doing a new thing; now it is springing up—do you not know about it? I will surely make a way in the desert, rivers in the wasteland.*

God is never too late! Pause and meditate upon this. He even rose Lazarus from the dead after four days. Maybe your situation looks the same, then I want to conclude by saying what Jesus said to His disciples when they thought it was too late ... *'And for your sake, I'm glad I wasn't there, because now you have another opportunity to see who I am so that you will learn to trust in me. Come, let's go and see him.'* (John 11:15 (TPT))

Lessons we can learn from Jesus:

1. Embrace the moment of pause in your life. Don't give in to frustration or disappointment. Use the opportunity to draw closer to God. He is never too late, never! His process can't be manipulated or short-circuited; He remains in control.

2. Endure through the trails and obstacles. Don't give up or pull back - persevere and work out your faith with fear and trembling until you receive your prize. James 1:12 (TPT) *'If your faith remains strong, even while surrounded by life's difficulties, you will continue to experience the untold blessings of God! True happiness comes as you pass the test with faith and receive the victorious crown of life promised to every lover of God!'*

3. Remain faithful and obedient. When you come to a place where you feel you have done all humanly possible - just stand, and remain standing! Continue to be faithful in doing well until the breakthrough appears.

4. Focus on Biblical examples and follow in their footsteps. *Hebrews 6:12 (TPT) So don't allow your hearts to grow dull or lose your enthusiasm but follow the example of those who fully received what God has promised because of their strong faith and patient endurance.*

5. Humble yourself and allow God to deal with pride and false motives. Ask the Holy Spirit to prune and form you into His image. (John 15:1-8)

6. Waiting builds our character and faith. Rom 5:3,4 (TPT) *'But that's not all! Even in times of trouble, we have joyful confidence, knowing that our pressures will develop patient endurance. And patient endurance will refine our character, and proven character leads us back to hope.'* Remember that God is a Father who delights in bestowing His blessings on His children. Imagine you are a child waiting for your birthday. You anticipate your gifts and birthday party with great excitement and delight. The longer the wait, the greater your anticipation and appreciation!

> **QUESTIONS:**
>
> 1. Testify about how how this chapter provided comfort in your life.
>
> 2. Is there a situation in your life that resembles Lazarus's life?
>
> 3. Spend time ministering and praying for one another about the above.

CONCLUSION

Hopefully, this manual has inspired you to look differently at the pauses in your life. May these times benefit your spiritual growth and cause you to bear abundant fruit to the glory of our King!

May you also become part of the mighty move of disciple-making that is upon the earth. It has always been the pattern in Biblical times and will remain this way until Jesus comes. May we also leave a legacy behind like Jesus did! While we pass the baton in discipleship-making, may we experience the fullness of joy promised for those who do the will of the Father.

John 4:36 (TPT) *'And everyone who reaps these souls for eternal life will receive a reward. And those who plant spiritual seeds and those who reap the harvest will celebrate together with great joy!'*

BIBLIOGRAPHY

The Scripture quotations identified as TPT are from *The Passion Translation*, copyrighted 2017 by Passion & Fire Ministries, Inc., and are used by Rick Meyers rick@e-sword.net. All rights reserved.

Verses marked NKJV are from *New King James Version,* copyrighted 1982 by Thomas Nelson. They were used with permission. All rights reserved.

Scripture quotations marked as ASV are from *American Standard Version,* published in 1901, public domain.

Scripture quotations marked as MKJV are from *Modern King James Version,* copyright@1962 – 1998, Jay P. Green, Sr. and are used by Rick Meyers rick@e-sword.net. All rights reserved.

Scripture quotations marked as TLV are from *Tree of Live Version,* copyright 2014, Messianic Jewish Family Bible Society and are used by permission of Rick Meyers rick@e-sword.net. All rights reserved.

Verses marked as NIV are from HOLY BIBLE: NEW INTERNATIONAL VERSION, Copyright @1973, 1978, 1984 by International Bible Society. They were used with the permission of Zondervan. All rights reserved.

No part of this publication may be reproduced or transmitted in any form or by any means – electronic, mechanical, photocopy, recording, or any other – except for brief quotations in printed reviews, without prior permission of the publisher.

www.ingramcontent.com/pod-product-compliance
Lightning Source LLC
Chambersburg PA
CBHW060351050426
42449CB00011B/2936